T0084513

# Simple Machines
# Pulleys

by Martha E. H. Rustad

CAPSTONE PRESS
a capstone imprint

Little Pebble is published by Capstone Press,
1710 Roe Crest Drive, North Mankato, Minnesota 56003
www.mycapstone.com

**Library of Congress Cataloging-in-Publication Data**
Names: Rustad, Martha E. H. (Martha Elizabeth Hillman), 1975– author.
Title: Pulleys / by Martha E.H. Rustad.
Description: North Mankato, Minnesota : Capstone Press, 2018. | Series:
    Little pebble. Simple machines | Audience: Ages 4–7.
Identifiers: LCCN 2017031576 (print) | LCCN 2017035877 (ebook) |
    ISBN 9781543500868 (eBook PDF) | ISBN 9781543500745 (hardcover) |
    ISBN 9781543500806 (paperback)
Subjects: LCSH: Pulleys—Juvenile literature.
Classification: LCC TJ1103 (ebook) | LCC TJ1103 .R87 2018 (print) | DDC
    621.8—dc23
LC record available at https://lccn.loc.gov/2017031576

**Editorial Credits**
Marissa Kirkman, editor; Kyle Grentz (cover) and Charmaine Whitman (interior), designers;
Jo Miller, media researcher; Katy LaVigne, production specialist

**Image Credits**
Alamy: VStock, 15; Capstone Studio: Karon Dubke, 11, 15 (inset), 17; Glow Images: Cultura RF/Henn Photography, 21; Shutterstock: BigIndianFootage, 13, bogdanhoda, 7, Carlos Caetano, cover, 1, Dutourdumonde Photography, 17 (inset), Feylite, 5, jayk67, 9, Lisa S., 19, Maliflower73, 19 (inset), Mathisa, 6, Monkey Business Images, 20, spetenfia, 22

**Design Elements**
Capstone

# Table of Contents

# Help with Work

Work is hard!

We need help.

Use a simple machine.

These tools help us work.

pulley

A pulley helps us move a load.

It lifts up heavy things.

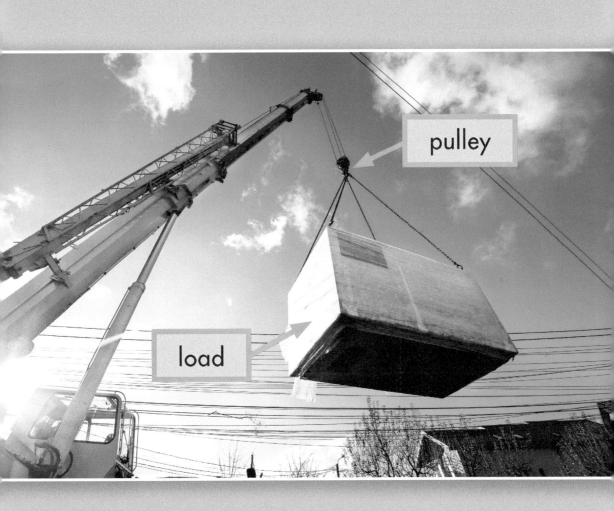

pulley

load

# Parts

See the rope.

It goes on a wheel.

Pull down.

The wheel turns.

The other side goes up.

wheel

Put a load on one side.

Pull.

Lift the load!

load

# Everyday Tools

A flagpole has a pulley.

Pull!

The flag rises.

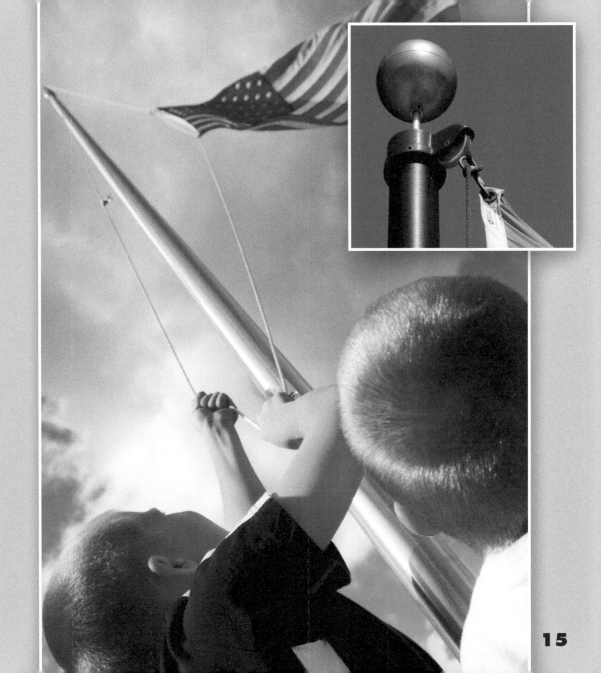

A bike has a pulley.

Pedal!

The bike moves.

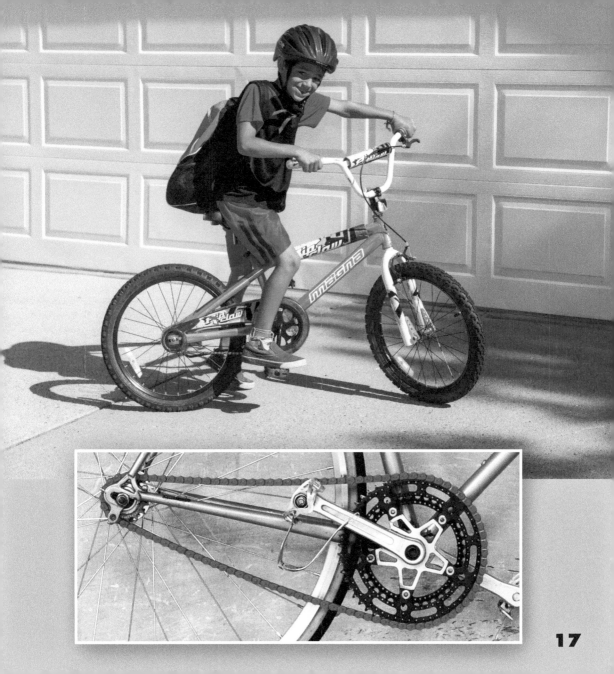

Blinds use pulleys.

Pull!

The blinds go up.

We use a simple machine.

It makes work easier and fun.

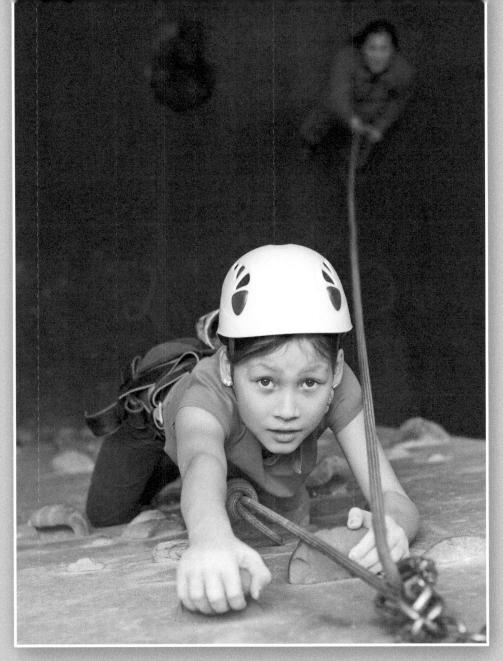

# Glossary

**blinds**—a covering for a window; a pulley helps to open and close blinds

**load**—an object that you want to move or lift

**simple machine**—a tool that makes it easier to move something

**wheel**—a round disc

**work**—a job that must be done

# Read More

La Machia, Dawn. *Pulleys at Work.* Zoom in on Simple Machines. New York: Enslow, 2016.

Schuh, Mari. *Raising a Bag of Toys: Pulley vs. Inclined Plane.* First Step Nonfiction: Simple Machines to the Rescue. Minneapolis: Lerner Publications, 2016.

Weakland, Mark. *Fred Flintstone's Adventures with Pulleys: Work Smarter, Not Harder.* Flintstones Explain Simple Machines. North Mankato, Minn.: Capstone Press, 2016.

# Internet Sites

Use FactHound to find Internet sites related to this book.

Visit www.facthound.com

Just type in 9781543500745 and go.

Check out projects, games and lots more at
**www.capstonekids.com**

# Critical Thinking Questions

1. What two parts does a pulley have?

2. What happens when you pull on one side of a pulley's rope?

3. What types of pulleys have you used?

# Index